THE SELF-HELP GUIDE FOR RETURNING CITIZENS

Pre-Release Planning for Post-Release Success

Author
TAM

Copyright © 2024 by: Tam Curley

All rights reserved. No part of this book may be used or reproduced by any means, graphic, electronic, or mechanical, including photocopying, recording, taping, or by any information storage retrieval system, without the written permission of the publisher except in the case of brief quotations embodied in critical articles and reviews.

TABLE OF CONTENTS

Preface 1

Chapter 1: A Fresh Start 3

Chapter 2: Your Career, Your Choice 20

Chapter 3: Yes, It Can Be Transferred! 23

Chapter 4: Exploring Job Zones 27

Chapter 5: Second-Chance Employers 31

Chapter 6: The Perfect Plan 37

Chapter 7: Exploring Training Post-Release 41

Chapter 8: Mental Challenges 45

PREFACE

---∞---

Tam is an experienced job developer who received offender workforce development specialist training credentials. She spent two (2) years working in a federal halfway house in Oakland, Calif., managing the employment program for returning citizens.

While working at the halfway house, Tam saw a need to help returning citizens prepare to meet the demands of the labor market and to assist them with their transition into full-time, sustainable employment or apprenticeship and/or educational training programs and suitable housing, thus helping reduce recidivism.

It was evident that returning citizens lacked job readiness and resources to ensure job readiness when they released to the halfway house. By the time returning citizens leave prison, it is already too late to begin thinking about what jobs, careers and/or educational pathways they wish to pursue.

Tam created this self-help guide to support returning citizens with setting goals & preparing for their future. This guide is the first of many, and it is not limited to returning citizens.

Why is Tam qualified to write this book?

While working at the halfway house, Tam had opportunities that allowed her to get into the grit of assisting returning citizens in more meaningful ways. Tam completed over 1600 hours of practicums and modules, resulting in obtaining the Offender Workforce Development Specialist certification. Following certification, Tam made connections and began collaborating with the U.S. Probation and Parole, the U.S. Pre-Trial Services, the U.S. Courts, the U.S. Department of Justice, the U.S. Bureau of Prison, as well as community, faith-based and non-profit organizations.

Tam collaborated with a re-entry representative from the Mayor's Office of the City of Oakland, and was invited to monthly networking meetings by the U.S. Probation District Office of California. The networking meetings involved diverse professionals dedicated to ensuring returning citizens' success post-release by discussing, planning and implementing ways to reduce recidivism.

A full-circle moment came years later when Tam was informed of an opportunity to serve as a panel grant reviewer for the U.S. Department of Labor's Employment and Training Administration. Tam began her first contract grant review in 2011, and continues to serve on an as-needed basis. Reviewers are responsible for reviewing, scoring and rating grantee applications. Grantees who receive federal financial assistance from the agency must adhere to providing employment and training services, they must incorporate pre-apprenticeship and apprenticeship opportunities as part of the services they offer, and they have an obligation to target hard-to-hire individuals, which includes ex-offenders, veterans, long-term unemployed, foster youth transitioning out of the foster care system, and other groups considered hard-to-hire.

CHAPTER 1
A FRESH START

Can you guess how many people fail to accomplish goals simply because they do not take the initiative to effectively plan? I do not have a specific number to give you, but my guess is the reason planners and planning committees exist is because it helps individuals and teams alike set goals, strategize and see the progress that has been made. When you think about planning, you should consider having plans ranging from 3 to 6 months for short-term goals, and 24 to 60 months for long-term goals. There reason hiring officials ask candidates where they see themselves in 5 to 10 years is because everyone should have set goals and plans mapped out at least 5 to 10 years ahead. Without a plan, stagnation and complacency becomes the norm. Deciding whether a plan is feasible depends on the individual, so one should not set unrealistic goals for themselves.

Going to prison is not something people look forward to, but it is inevitable when they have committed crimes. Life does not end on the first day of prison. It begins. It is a time to familiarize yourself with people who can assist you while incarcerated. Many individuals enter prison without a release plan, maybe because they have long prison sentences, or maybe because no one ever told them to create a plan when entering prison—they are only told to quickly get [it] together for their fast-approaching release date, which is usually too late. Returning citizens without a realistic pre-release plan will have some difficulty post-release. The amount of time a person spends in prison is usually more than enough time to fully prepare for their transition from prison to the halfway house, and eventually home.

Having a release plan is essential, and ensures you are successful upon release, as opposed to not having a plan and risking recidivism.

Recidivism (re-entering prison) is hurtful to your loved ones. Mothers, fathers, children, grandparents, and friends are on the journey to [freedom] alongside you. It is up to you to ensure that you are not part of the statistical number of people who return to prison each year.

Successful release planning includes understanding your conditions of release which details the limitations you have as far as employment is concerned, if in fact limitations exit. If your conditions of release do not detail your employment terms, you should ask your probation officer to help. You will likely not be assigned a probation officer until a few months prior to your release date, and if that is the case, you can speak to staff at the prison to help you so that you are not in a training program your conditions of release will likely say you cannot do upon release. It takes time to research, and may require you to reach out to family and friends to help you get clear and concise answers before deciding on a career training path, if you are not able to return to what you were doing prior to incarceration. It is common for people who go to prison to complete their prison sentence with more job training and relevant skills than they had prior to incarceration. Many federal prisons offer training programs to all incarcerated individuals, but those individuals must be eligible to participate in those programs. If you are lucky enough to start and complete a training program while incarcerated, that says to an uncertain employer, "they mastered a skill we can use, therefore, I am willing to take a chance on them." Although many laws remain outdated, there are laws in place to ensure incarcerated men and women receive skills training while incarcerated. Begin your own pre-release plan below. Complete the pages in this guide within the first thirty (30) days of incarceration. It is okay to ask for help completing the pages, but remember, it is your responsibility to ensure the research is beneficial to your unique situation.

Put plenty of thought and time into completing all pages. Do not just write something without substance. Make sure to include information and resources that can assist you and help you implement a pre-release plan. Make sure your plan is reasonable, attainable and sustainable.

List the names of training instructors at the prison.

What are the training programs and certifications offered at the prison? Identify the ones you are interested in.

Continuation Page…

Continuation Page…

What are the requirements (or limitations) for the training program(s) you chose? Write the name of the training program and certification you can/will earn, program requirements and limitations that may exist.

Continuation Page…

Continuation Page…

Is there a waiting list for the training program(s) you chose? If so, write it down and include your position or number on the waiting list as well as the date you expect to start and finish the program.

Continuation Page…

Continuation Page…

Consider the city and state where you will live. List in-demand jobs for that geographic area that requires little to no education. Use the Bureau of Labor Statistics website (https://www.bls.gov/ooh/) to reference the Occupational Outlook Handbook and generate a list of occupations.

Continuation Page…

Continuation Page…

Identify people within the community who can assist you with obtaining employment. These people can be friends, family, previous employers, co-workers, and community leaders.

Continuation Page…

CHAPTER 2
YOUR CAREER, YOUR CHOICE

Before you go too deep looking at jobs, job zones, and in-demand jobs, you should have a clear understanding of what careers and job functions interest you. People tend to thrive in careers they choose, and fail at jobs they do not have a genuine interest in. Having a criminal history should not force you into choosing a dead-end job that you will eventually leave. Keep in mind that if you have committed white-collar crimes, you may have to explore different career paths because of your conditions of release. If you have worked in high-paying fields, you most likely will not settle for anything not similarly situated. You can analyze what interests you by looking at the Interest Profiler here: https://www.mynextmove.org/explore/ip

Make a list of your top career interests. List as many or as few as you like.

Continuation Page…

CHAPTER 3
YES, IT CAN BE TRANSFERRED!

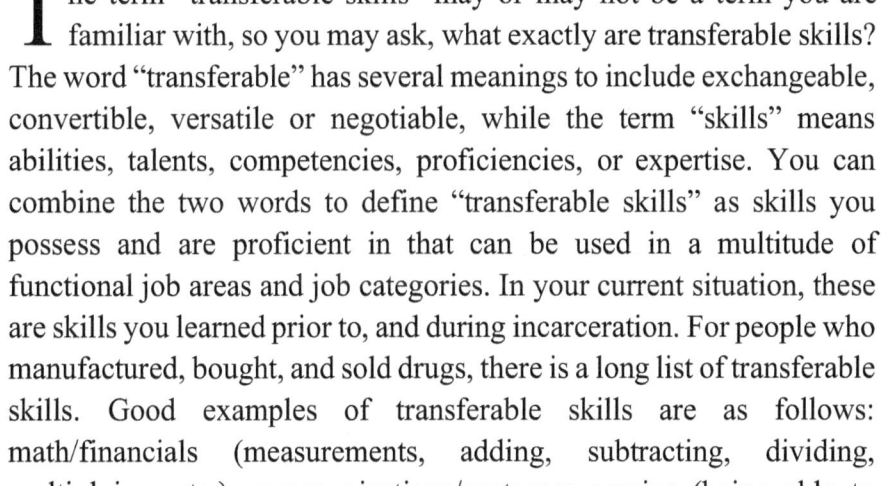

The term "transferable skills" may or may not be a term you are familiar with, so you may ask, what exactly are transferable skills? The word "transferable" has several meanings to include exchangeable, convertible, versatile or negotiable, while the term "skills" means abilities, talents, competencies, proficiencies, or expertise. You can combine the two words to define "transferable skills" as skills you possess and are proficient in that can be used in a multitude of functional job areas and job categories. In your current situation, these are skills you learned prior to, and during incarceration. For people who manufactured, bought, and sold drugs, there is a long list of transferable skills. Good examples of transferable skills are as follows: math/financials (measurements, adding, subtracting, dividing, multiplying, etc.), communications/customer service (being able to speak to and understand the wants and needs of customers), and chemistry (being able to mix safe ingredients to make new products that can help maximize profits), per se. For people who stole, and resold goods, sales and marketing may offer relevant transferable skills.

Are there volunteer or lead roles you can secure at the prison that will allow you to gain transferable skills? If so, identify and list them below.

This is where you should think about, and generate a list of transferable skills. Do not limit yourself while making this list because it will be useful when creating your resume.

Continuation Page....

CHAPTER 4
EXPLORING JOB ZONES

Your career interests should be clearly defined by now, and if so, you should begin focusing on, and exploring job zones. It is important to prevent as many barriers to employment post-release as possible. Before you begin a new career, it is important to understand job zones as you examine what fields require little to no training, and which fields require extensive training.

Call it luck or a blessing, but some employers will hire you with no experience, if they like you. Let's ignore that fact, and get you started thinking about the list you generated above. Job zones start with jobs and titles that require little to no training and experience, and those that require extensive training and experience. Think about the list above and what you identified as having a genuine interest.

How much training is needed for a particular job? Use this website: https://www.mynextmove.org/find/zone and make your job zones list below by identifying jobs and job zones.

Continuation Page…

Continuation Page…

CHAPTER 5
SECOND-CHANCE EMPLOYERS

You have made it to the [somewhat] difficult part, which is deciding where you want to work, and where your criminal history will not be a barrier for you. Even if you have done due diligence by identifying and completing a training program, have a good understanding of your skills and interests, have identified job zones, and know where you want to work, you should understand that there are a lot of employers who will not consider hiring you for no other reason than your criminal past. There are a multitude of community-based, faith-based and non-profit organizations that have partnership agreements with employers that will hire you regardless of your criminal record. This section, by far, is one of the most important sections to complete. It will prevent you from going in circles trying to convince employers to hire you based on your qualifications, education, and experience. Do not limit what you include in this section, and you should be mindful of the work you have done in the previous sections.

Tip: Check with your local and state government because many offer second-chance programs, and have ban-the-box laws.

If you live in the **State of Texas, Dallas County** has adopted a ban-the-box policy (see here):
https://www.dallascounty.org/departments/HR/onboarding/ban-the-box.php

Dallas City Hall Small Business Center has a FreshStart Employment Program:
https://dallascityhall.com/departments/sbcworkforcedev/Pages/FreshStart- Employment-Program-Workforce.aspx

National Reentry Resource Center
www.nationalreentryresourcecenter.org/second- chance-act/sca-grantee-program-map. The program is funded, and administered by the Department of Justice/Office of Justice Programs/Bureau of Justice Assistance.

The Manufacturing Institute https://themanufacturinginstitute.org/ is a program that was launched to encourage second-chance hiring. If you know of an employer who could benefit from second-chance hiring, tell them to sign up here.

For a list of fair hiring and second-chance employers in the network, visit:

https://jailstojobs.org/

The Fair Chance Corporate Cohort is an organization focused on fair-chance hiring, and expands employment opportunities for people with criminal records: https://info.jff.org/fairchancecohort.

The Potter's House has a program, T.O.R.I. (Texas Offender's Reentry Initiative) which assists men and women across the state of Texas: https://medc-tori.org/.

Use the next few pages to search and identify second-chance employers. This list could vary greatly and may not be relevant to everyone simply because of different geographic locations. Start making a list of places that will hire you regardless of your criminal record.

List as many [felon-friendly] employers as you can.

Continuation Page…

Continuation Page...

Continuation Page…

CHAPTER 6
THE PERFECT PLAN

It is close to your release date, and you are nervous and excited because you will soon see [freedom] as you remember it. You hear that when you arrive at the halfway house, you must find a full-time job within fifteen (15) business days or risk returning to custody. You hear that when you arrive at the halfway house, you will have to pay the facility a mandatory twenty-five percent (25%) of your gross income. You hear that you cannot be self-employed, nor can you work for friends and family. You hear that once you secure full-time employment, you can complete your transition from prison by way of the halfway house, on home confinement. The things you hear are true, but you may or may not hear about the real barriers you may face as it relates to identifying documents, if you do not obtain them pre-release. The identifying documents include the following: current copy of your state driver's license or ID, social security card, and birth certificate. You will likely spend the first week going through intake. Intake, put simply, is facility orientation: meeting with your case manager, learning the rules of the facility, learning about community and recreation time, job-searching, visitation, and so much more. Once the intake process is complete, you can start the process of applying for a new state driver's license or ID, social security card, and birth certificate. Without identifying documents, everything else becomes an obstacle and can be frustrating, especially considering the fact that you are not allowed to have a personal vehicle while living at the halfway house. Returning citizens who are released from minimum-security facilities where better pre-release preparation was provided, will experience a smoother transition.

You may or may not already have your state driver's license or ID, social security card, birth certificate, a support group, money to buy personal care items, and clothing you owned prior to incarceration that you can still wear. If you do not have the aforementioned items, the first weeks can be cumbersome.

You soon begin to realize that the so-called friends who committed crimes alongside you are no longer around. Everyone who was saying, "free my n!gga," are either deceased, incarcerated, down on their luck or avoiding you altogether because they were never really [down] with you. Maybe they just don't care about you and your successful transition back into society as a law-abiding citizen because now, they don't have you to participate in illegal activities. You cannot change things from the past, you cannot change people, you cannot force or even beg people to help you, and most importantly, you cannot dwell on what you no longer have. You have 4 to 6 months, or maybe longer, and the only thing you really have is—you. Your focus should be making it to the halfway house, and once you figure out what you have or don't have, you should identify available resources. In the beginning, you may have feelings of despair, and the only thing you can think about is going back [in] because it was easier when your entire life was planned out for you, and controlled by someone other than yourself. It may have been easier, but time did not stop. You missed important milestones: the birth of your first-born child, the passing of your grandmother, your younger brother's graduation, your baby's first steps, and so many other things. So, yes, being [free] is better than being incarcerated—or at least it should be. Before you begin your job search, and immediately after you have completed intake at the halfway house, you must figure some things out, and it needs to happen quickly.

Do you have identifying documents (state driver's license or ID, social security card, and birth certificate)? If not, what do you need to do to get them? Identify family and friends who can help you approximately 3 to 6 months prior to your release date.

Do you have proper clothing to wear for job searches and interviews? If not, do you have people who can help you? If not, do you know what community-based, faith-based and non-profit organizations can help for free? Identify the ones near the halfway house where you will spend the next few months.

CHAPTER 7
EXPLORING TRAINING POST-RELEASE

If you were not successful in completing a training program while incarcerated, you may want to consider applying to apprenticeship training programs externally. There are numerous programs across the U.S. that pays the apprentice to learn a trade while providing them with nationally recognized credentials. Registered apprenticeship programs are vetted, approved and validated by the U.S. Department of Labor or a state apprenticeship agency. As a side note, if you know any businesses that are not registered to provide apprenticeship training, but you want them to offer training, you can tell them about the benefits of becoming a RAP (Registered Apprenticeship Program) which includes free technical assistance, standards set forth by the federal government to ensure the program meets national standards, and tax credits available to the RAP. The Apprenticeship.gov website provides more detailed information about registered apprenticeship programs, and provides a list of training opportunities in advanced manufacturing, agriculture, construction, cybersecurity, education, energy, financial services, healthcare, hospitality, information technology, telecom and transportation. Returning citizens can click on the industry of interest and download the resource guide which teaches about apprenticeships in a specific industry. Additionally, it shows high-demand apprenticeship occupations within a particular industry. Aside from the Bureau of Labor Statistics website, Apprenticeship.gov is a good place to assess and cross reference in-demand jobs in a specific geographic area.

Make a list of apprenticeship programs (post-release) that interest you and list the requirements of each.

Continuation Page…

Continuation Page…

CHAPTER 8
MENTAL CHALLENGES

This very important closing chapter provides resources to help you deal with your mental health needs. Mental challenges can hit hard without you realizing it. You may have never dealt with stress, and you may have never seen a therapist because you always [figured things out], but the transition from prison back to the community can be a stressful process, and could have a tremendous impact on you both physically and mentally. What you need to do is focus on your overall health, if the transition becomes too much to manage. Going back to prison will not solve any problems, because at some point in the future, you will have to restart the process, and may face similar obstacles all over again. What happens when you need mental health services, but do not have the financial means to pay for this type of service? You can start by trying to address certain issues on your own by visiting the following websites and downloading free worksheets and interactive videos:

https://www.therapistaid.com and

https://mindremakeproject.org/free- printables/ (free pintables) and https://mindremakeproject.org/resources/#Resource_Links_for_Finding_Help (resources for legal help, free HIV testing, medication assistance and so much more). If self-help exercises are not helping, and you need to locate a treatment facility, please visit https://findtreatment.samhsa.gov/. For more urgent concerns, you may call the Suicide Prevention Lifeline at 1-800-273-TALK (8255), the Disaster Distress Helpline, at 1-800-985-5990 or text TalkWithUs at 66746.

www.ingramcontent.com/pod-product-compliance
Lightning Source LLC
Chambersburg PA
CBHW070108100426
42743CB00012B/2689